Hazelden

A Lecture Series

THE DISEASE OF ADDICTION

Symptoms and Phases

Bruce Larson, MA, LADC

HAZELDEN®

Hazelden
Center City, Minnesota 55012-0176

1-800-328-9000
1-651-213-4590 (Fax)
www.hazelden.org

About the Author

A nationally certified alcohol and drug counselor, Bruce Larson is currently supervisor of Hazelden's counselor training programs. He has advocated for professional standards in counseling and counseling education for over twenty years through board participation at the state and national level.

Editor's Note

The Twelve Steps are reprinted with permission of Alcoholics Anonymous World Services, Inc. Permission to reprint the Twelve Steps does not mean that AA has reviewed or approved the contents of this publication, nor that AA agrees with the views expressed herein. AA is a program of recovery from alcoholism *only*—use of the Twelve Steps in connection with programs and activities which are patterned after AA, but which address other problems, or in any other non-AA context, does not imply otherwise.

All the stories in this workbook are based on actual experiences. The names and details have been changed to protect the privacy of the people involved. In some cases, composites have been created.

INTRODUCTION

Understanding addiction strains our sense of logic. How can individuals not see the consequences of their use when it is clear to others? What motivates people to continue to use alcohol and other drugs even though it may cost them a relationship, a job, or their own self-respect? Why does someone return to alcohol and other drugs even after making a personal commitment not to use again?

Facing the possibility that you might be an alcoholic or dependent on other drugs can also be painful, overwhelming, and confusing. Facing a relapse can be just as scary.

You and your loved ones probably have struggled with these difficult questions and more. Facing the possibility that you might be an alcoholic or dependent on other drugs can also be painful, overwhelming, and confusing. Facing a relapse can be just as scary.

To help you better understand addiction and its phases, this workbook is divided into three sections: (1) addiction as a disease, (2) key elements of the disease, and (3) phases of addiction. In each section, writing exercises and questions help you to think about how the information applies to your life.

ADDICTION AS A DISEASE

The earliest known attempt to define alcoholism occurred in the late 1700s. Father of American psychiatry and signer of the *Declaration of Independence* Benjamin Rush described drunkenness in an essay as a progressive medical condition. In 1939, Dr. William D. Silkworth, whose letters appear in "The Doctor's Opinion" in *Alcoholics Anonymous* (the Big Book), wrote that the action of alcohol on alcoholics is a manifestation of an allergy and that the phenomenon of craving experienced by alcoholics never occurs in the average drinker. Finally, in 1956, the American Medical Association (AMA) declared that alcoholism is a disease and that it is treatable.

The recognition that addiction to other drugs, besides alcohol, is a disease has only recently received more widespread credibility.

Dr. Alan Leshner, director of the National Institute of Drug Abuse (NIDA), reported on scientific evidence that the abuse of alcohol and other drugs actually changes the brain's chemistry and structure to create what he calls "a disease state." He described addiction as "fundamentally a brain disease."[1]

Many people still struggle to accept that addiction is a disease even though the AMA, researchers, and scientific evidence define it as such. For hundreds of years, alcoholics and drug addicts have been viewed and portrayed as bad, weak-willed, immoral, or criminal. Society and the media continue to define addicts in these ways. These attitudes create powerful and long-lasting images that are difficult to change.

In some ways, these negative views of alcoholics and addicts are understandable. People see the pain and suffering that individuals using alcohol and drugs can cause to themselves and others. They do not understand why alcoholics or addicts do not simply quit or use moderately, why they can't start acting as responsible, moral citizens and family members. However, it is key to our own recovery that we understand addiction as a disease and not a moral failure. When we accept that addiction is a disease, we are more likely to take the steps necessary for recovery.

It is key to our own recovery that we understand addiction as a disease and not a moral failure.

Abusing alcohol and other drugs compels us to act against our own will and values, risk important relationships, and shirk significant responsibilities. These are signs that we have a disease and need help, not that we have a moral failing.

[1] *The Hijacked Brain*, in Moyers on Addiction: Close to Home collection, Films for Humanities, 1998, videocassette.

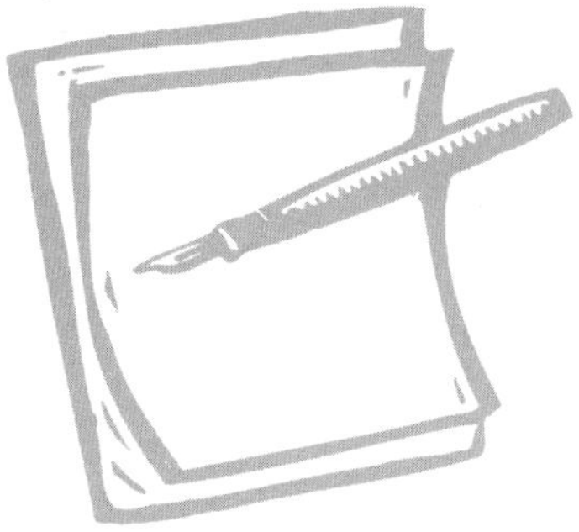

Take a minute to reflect on the beliefs you and others in your life have about your drinking and drug use.

Members of my family believe that if I just tried harder or if I cared more that I would have quit using or drinking.

1	2	3	4
Not true at all	*Somewhat true*	*Mostly true*	*Painfully true*

Some friends see my continued use of alcohol and other drugs as a weakness in me.

1	2	3	4
Not true at all	*Somewhat true*	*Mostly true*	*Painfully true*

I should have been able to stop drinking or using on my own.

1	2	3	4
Not true at all	*Somewhat true*	*Mostly true*	*Painfully true*

I have a no-fault disease that I could not control.

1	2	3	4
I don't think this	*I'm beginning to think this, more and more*	*I think this*	*I'm convinced*

Remember, it is natural for us, our families, and our friends to have mixed views and feelings about recognizing addiction as a disease. Yet, if we hold on to negative images of addiction and blame ourselves, we will risk our recovery. We are not bad people. We are good people with a bad disease.

KEY ELEMENTS OF THE DISEASE

The American Society of Addiction Medicine and the National Council on Alcoholism and Drug Dependence recently defined *alcoholism* as "a *primary, chronic* disease with *genetic,* psychosocial, and environmental factors influencing its development and manifestations. The disease is often *progressive* and *fatal.* It is characterized by continuous or periodic impaired control over use, preoccupation with use, use despite adverse consequences, and distortions in thinking, most notably denial" (italics added).[2]

In this section, we will look at each of the five key terms italicized in the definition above and use them to discuss the concept of addiction. In order to live responsibly with the disease, it is important that you understand the nature of addiction as *primary, chronic, genetic, progressive,* and *fatal.*

Primary: It's the Number One Problem in Your Life

Recognizing addiction as a primary disease is an important key that can open the door of recovery. *Primary* means that addiction is *not* a symptom of an underlying problem, such as depression, anxiety, or low self-esteem, but a separate disease with its own course and complications.

Recognizing addiction as a primary disease is an important key that can open the door of recovery.

Many people who drink or use drugs do not believe they have a primary disease. Instead, they think that they drink or use drugs because of "other" issues. They may think they drink because they are depressed about a painful relationship or use drugs just to relieve the stress of a hard day at work. Looking at the problem this way only leads to continued drinking, drug use, or relapse. Let's look at Jill's history to explore this more closely.

[2] This definition was prepared by the Joint Committee to Study the Definition and Criteria for the Diagnosis of Alcoholism of the National Council on Alcoholism and Drug Dependence [NCADD] and the American Society of Addiction Medicine [ASAM]. It was approved by the Board of Directors of NCADD on 3 February 1990 and the Board of Directors of ASAM on 25 February 1990. Appeared in the *Journal of the American Medical Association (JAMA)* 268, no. 8:1012–14.

JILL

Jill is a twenty-eight-year-old married woman who is in treatment for the first time. Her mother is alcoholic, and she has an aunt and uncle on her father's side with a history of alcohol- and drug-related problems. Jill sees her drinking as different from her mother's. Jill thinks she drinks because she's overweight, depressed, and anxious. Jill also has used Xanax daily for the past year. She feels it helped relieve her anxiety. Jill was upset when the doctor told her she needed to be medically withdrawn from it to avoid any chance of seizure.

Like many of us, Jill fell into the trap of thinking that her drinking is not the problem. She is convinced that she would drink less if she could lose weight and get help with her depression and anxiety. Worse yet, Jill thinks Xanax, and probably alcohol, will partly solve her problems. Why didn't Jill see that her primary problem is addiction?

Jill probably felt depressed and anxious about her weight and body image for a long time, even before alcohol or Xanax became a problem. In fact, she never saw alcohol as a problem. Drinking gave her energy and helped her eat less. Since alcohol relieved her depression and anxiety, how could it be bad for her, she wondered?

Jill overlooked how her family's history of addiction put her more at risk. She relied more and more on alcohol for temporary relief, and she didn't know that her drinking had changed her brain structure and chemistry. Because she was constantly using alcohol, her brain stopped making the natural chemicals that helped her feel good. Over time, her dependence on alcohol made her depression and anxiety worse. Jill's increased sense of "dis-ease" reinforced her view that depression and anxiety were her problems, not alcohol.

She went to a doctor with her concerns, not mentioning her alcohol use, and was given Xanax. It eased her anxiety. As with alcohol, she relied on Xanax more and more to cope, without realizing it, too, was addictive.

Jill's situation illustrates the primary nature of addiction. Ironically, the very drugs that initially give us relief, in time, create a cycle of dependency. Once the brain adapts, a person needs more alcohol and drugs to feel better, which damages the brain further and increases the need for more chemicals. A vicious cycle is in place. At this point, addiction becomes a separate problem with its own destructive course. If we think that resolving other issues will allow us to drink or use drugs normally, we are tragically mistaken.

I believe that I have a primary disease.

1	2	3	4
I don't believe it	*I have mixed beliefs*	*I'm getting there*	*I have no doubt*

Recognizing that addiction is primary, however, does not mean that resolving other issues is unimportant to recovery. Sometimes, issues like depression, high blood pressure, sleep disturbances, and relationship problems improve or disappear with recovery. Other times, these problems persist or worsen. They do not go away with recovery. The key is to get help for these issues while staying focused on recovery from our addiction.

Most of us have felt that our drinking or other drug use would not be a problem if we could just resolve certain situations or feelings. Where do you stand on this issue?

In the past, I felt my drinking or other drug use would not be a problem if I could just do the following:

1.

2.

I now realize that my alcohol and drug use is a separate problem.

1	2	3	4
I don't believe it	*I have mixed beliefs*	*I'm getting there*	*I have no doubt*

Chronic: It's Forever

The word *chronic* comes from the Greek myth of Chronos who was the god of time. Chronic means "lasting forever." Diabetes, heart disease, and emphysema are chronic diseases—so is addiction. Bob's story helps illustrate the chronic nature of addiction.

BOB

Bob is a fifty-five-year-old, divorced father of two adult children and is in treatment for the fourth time. In Bob's first treatments, he thought he was different from others. He didn't drink as much or as often as his peers in treatment or the people he heard speak in Alcoholics Anonymous (AA). Bob had fewer consequences from his drinking and no medical complications. Bob did not believe he was alcoholic and returned to drinking within weeks after completing his first two treatments. His third treatment was a result of a family intervention. Bob, now admitting to his alcoholism, stayed sober for five years, not wanting to lose his family. Bob thought he had beat his addiction and could safely drink again. But his drinking began to progress rapidly. His wife divorced him. His job is at risk. He is isolated from his family and friends. He is depressed, confused, demoralized, and resentful.

Despite five years of sobriety, Bob was not "cured." No alcoholic or addict is ever cured of addiction. People in Twelve Step programs describe themselves as "recovering" not "recovered" from alcoholism or drug dependency; they do this to remind themselves that they are never cured once and for all. Our disease is always with us. We cannot cure ourselves, but we can heal through daily recovery.

This means we need to consider each day how to live effectively as a recovering alcoholic or addict. We are not alone in this. People with heart disease, diabetes, and other chronic conditions do this as well. In order to live alcohol- and drug-free, we need to make physical, social, emotional, and spiritual lifestyle changes that support recovery.

Some alcoholics or addicts dream that someday they will be able to drink or use normally. On page 30 of the Big Book we read: "The idea that somehow, someday he [or she] will control and enjoy . . . drinking is the great obsession of every abnormal drinker." Many chemically dependent people don't know that they have a powerful and long-lived emotional memory of intoxication or addiction etched deep in their brain. Drinking or using again triggers this memory, setting the addictive process back in motion. Accepting we have a chronic disease means that we believe we will never be able to use alcohol or other drugs normally.

"The idea that somehow, someday he [or she] will control and enjoy . . . drinking is the great obsession of every abnormal drinker."

– The Big Book

Do you believe that you will never be able to use alcohol or other drugs normally?

1	2	3	4
No	*I'm not sure*	*I'm getting there*	*I have no doubt*

Briefly describe why you think this way.

Genetic: It's Likely You Inherited It

Addiction is partly genetic, though psychosocial and environmental factors such as depression, anxiety, traumatic events, and family dynamics play a part in how it develops and shows itself. Genetics has as much to do with addiction as it does in other chronic illnesses such as heart disease, cancer, and diabetes.

Have you ever considered that your genes might have made it more likely that you would become alcoholic or addicted to another drug? There is strong evidence that this is true. Studies that have looked at differences in brain waves, sensitivity to alcohol, and effects of alcohol on hormones in the blood all point to genetic differences in people who are addicted.

Adoption studies provide the strongest evidence that addiction is passed on to us through genetics. Adopted sons and daughters of alcoholic parents have a greater risk (four times higher) of becoming alcoholic (even *without* exposure to their alcoholic parents) than children of nonalcoholics. If you have a parent or close relative who is addicted, you probably were born with a reduced supply of and ability to use natural brain chemicals or neurotransmitters like dopamine, enkephalins, and serotonin—natural chemicals that help you feel good. Because we don't have enough of these natural chemicals, it is difficult for us to experience a sense of well-being. We have found that alcohol or other drugs give us this "up" feeling—euphoria—caused by a complex communication process between our brain cells and neurotransmitters that result in the release of dopamine in the pleasure center of our brain.

If you have a parent or close relative who is addicted, you probably were born with a reduced supply of and ability to use natural brain chemicals . . . that help you feel good.

Some of us know addiction runs deeply in our families. Others may not. Many families avoid talking about Uncle Joe's drinking or Grandma's use of tranquilizers and sleeping pills. Sometimes, they just see a family member's drinking and drug use as normal.

Does your family history put you at risk for addiction?

1	2	3
Yes	*No*	*Not sure*

If so, name your family members who have had difficulties with or regularly used alcohol or other drugs, including prescriptions.

1. .... 3. ....

2. .... 4. ....

Others: ....

Progressive: It Gets Worse, Not Better

Another characteristic of the disease is that it is progressive. This simply means that the disease persists and worsens over time. The following description of John gives us a sense of the progressive nature of addiction.

JOHN

John is forty-eight and recently sought help for his crack cocaine use. John has no family history of addiction. He experimented with alcohol and other drugs in college without major consequences. After college, alcohol and other drugs took a backseat to John's marriage and career, but he continued to drink socially, smoke marijuana, and snort cocaine on occasion. He has been very successful in business the last twenty years. About two years ago, John started to smoke crack. Recently, his binges have been more frequent, longer, and have caused more problems at work and home. He has cheated on his wife. Two recent seizures, increased paranoia, suicidal thoughts, and the threat of losing his family convinced him that he needs to quit smoking crack. However, since he considers his drinking as social, it is difficult for him to see the need not to drink.

You might ask what caused John's drug use to progress so rapidly in the last two years? How quickly or how slowly progression occurs is complex. Individual vulnerability, home environment, attitudes toward alcohol and other drug use, life events, emotional and spiritual resources, and history of personal failures and successes all affect the rate of the disease's progression. The power of the drug, the frequency and strength of the dosage, and the speed at which the drug gets to the brain influence the progression.

In John's case, both his increased use and his personal problems indicated that his disease had progressed. As John lost control of his use of crack, more consequences occurred. As more consequences occurred, John used more crack to reduce stress, numb pain, and feel better. With continued use, crack "worked" less and less and instead produced lingering unpleasant feelings, which only required more use. By repeatedly injuring his brain with cocaine, marijuana, alcohol, and eventually crack, John's brain changed, leaving him more and more dependent on drugs to feel better.

This is not speculation. Through the use of amazing technology, researchers have captured images of the differences between a brain on drugs and a brain after abstinence from drugs. These images also show how the brain changes with repeated use of alcohol and other drugs. The brain is incredibly complex. Though we have a lot more to learn, this research proves that drugs change the brain's chemistry and structure.

We know that no matter what the addictive substance—alcohol, amphetamines, sedatives, or narcotics—all drugs activate the neurotransmitter dopamine deep in the reward center of the brain. When we keep using addictive chemicals, our brains begin to need the drugs more, and they stop producing the natural chemicals that give us a sense of well-being—eventually we need to use chemicals just to feel right. The same drugs that make us feel euphoric, excited, and free of physical and emotional pain eventually steal our brain's normal ability to sense pleasure.

The same drugs that make us feel euphoric, excited, and free of physical and emotional pain eventually steal our brain's normal ability to sense pleasure.

Do you believe that abuse of alcohol and other drugs has caused your brain to change negatively?

1	2	3	4
No	*I'm not sure*	*I'm getting there*	*I have no doubt*

Do you accept that you have a progressive disease?

1	2	3	4
No	*I'm not sure*	*I'm getting there*	*I have no doubt*

Briefly describe why you think this way.

Fatal: It Can Kill You

You probably think of inoperable cancer or severe emphysema as fatal diseases, but not addiction. However, addiction can be as fatal. Toxic effects of constant alcohol use can cause death through medical complications, such as liver disease and heart failure. Other addiction-related causes of death include strokes, heart attacks, and respiratory arrest. Most deaths related to addiction involve a traumatic event.

Many of us know this firsthand. We have lost family members or friends as a result of alcohol- and drug-related medical problems, car accidents, or suicide. You may have had serious suicidal thoughts or have attempted suicide. Maybe you have been involved in domestic violence where you or someone you know was at great risk for permanent injury or death. Perhaps you have lost friends or acquaintances to a drug overdose or AIDS.

Addiction is a very serious disease. It is so powerful it often overrides our instinct of survival. We continue to use despite grave risks. How has the fatal characteristic of addiction touched your life?

Do you know of anyone who has died directly or indirectly because of addiction? If it is not too emotional to do so, describe what happened.

Describe two ways your alcohol and drug use has put you in "harm's way."

1.

2.

PHASES OF ADDICTION

In the early 1950s, E. M. Jellinek, a pioneer in alcoholism research, described three phases of alcohol and drug addiction: prodromal, crucial, and chronic. How quickly a person progresses through each phase varies. Individual vulnerabilities, drug of choice, frequency, amount and method of use, gender, psychosocial and environmental factors all make a difference.

For instance, an unemployed heroin addict who has to account to no one might progress rapidly through each phase, whereas a mother with young children who might conceal her drinking by waiting until the kids are out of the house or in bed may progress more slowly through each phase.

How quickly a person progresses through each phase varies.

In the remainder of this workbook the three phases of the disease will be described. You will be asked to think about which warning signs you have experienced in each phase. If you honestly cannot think of ways you have experienced these symptoms of addiction, consider asking your family, friends, or a counselor what they have seen. Asking other recovering alcoholics and addicts can also be helpful.

Prodromal Phase

Prodromal means "giving warning." In the prodromal phase, there are four classic warning signs or symptoms of alcohol and drug addiction. They are (1) using alcohol or other drugs as "rewards," (2) tolerance, (3) concealing use, and (4) preoccupation. These symptoms, explored in detail below, demonstrate or reflect our need for and dependence on alcohol and other drugs to feel good.

Using Alcohol or Other Drugs as Rewards

Each of us responds to drugs in a different way. Maybe drinking helped you to relax and feel calm. Slugging down shots of whiskey might have made you confident. Perhaps using drugs gave you a sense of power, happiness, or energy. Maybe you tried to numb physical or emotional pain. No matter what the feeling, it was rewarding.

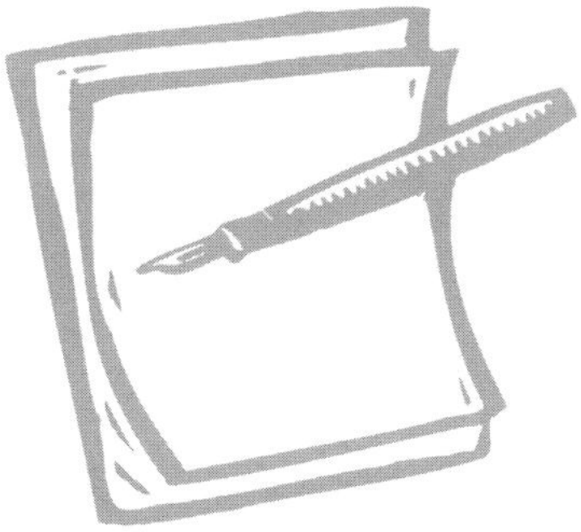

What three drugs have been most rewarding to you?

1. .... 2. .... 3. ....

Describe what the rewarding feeling was for each drug you listed.

1. ....

2. ....

3. ....

Tolerance

Tolerance means that we eventually need to use more alcohol or other drugs to achieve a rewarding effect or that the drug's effect is less rewarding when we use the same amount. Have you noticed your tolerance of alcohol and other drugs change over time? Sometimes people drink more, more often, or consume stronger drinks. Some people might begin to combine drugs, such as alcohol and a tranquilizer. Others might increase their dose by smoking or injecting drugs.

List which drugs you developed tolerance to and provide an example. Example: At first two drinks relaxed me. Now it takes four to relax me.

1.

2.

3.

Concealing Use

As tolerance increases, we often feel self-conscious about our use. We don't want others to know how often we are using or how much money we spend on alcohol or other drugs. Whether you are an intravenous user who conceals track marks from friends, or a parent who tries to keep your kids from knowing, concealing alcohol and drug use is a warning sign that your addiction is progressing.

List two ways you have recently concealed your use and from whom.

1.

2.

Preoccupation

Preoccupation means we spend more time and energy on planning and obtaining alcohol and other drugs, using and recovering from their effects, and thinking about the next time we can drink or use. Preoccupation steals time from important areas of our lives. Other examples of preoccupation include going to different doctors or pharmacies for prescriptions, arranging your work schedule around your drinking, or calling in sick because of drinking or drug use.

Give two examples of how you have spent energy planning alcohol or drug use.

1.

2.

Name two ways alcohol and other drugs have taken your time and energy away from important activities, responsibilities, or relationships.

1.

2.

Alcohol or drug use has taken too important of a place in my life.

1	2	3	4
Not really	*Maybe a little*	*Only recently*	*Absolutely*

Crucial Phase

The crucial phase begins when we start losing control over our use. Our alcohol and drug use increases and begins to complicate our lives even more. In this phase, we minimize, justify, or deny our use to ourselves and others. We blame other people or situations for our alcohol or drug use and related problems.

The crucial phase is characterized by four major symptoms: (1) impaired control, (2) continued use despite harmful consequences, (3) unsuccessful attempts to limit or stop use, and (4) alcohol- and drug-centered behavior. These symptoms signal further progression of our disease. The questions below encourage you to reflect on these crucial phase symptoms for the last twelve months of your using.

In this phase, we minimize, justify, or deny our use to ourselves and others. We blame other people or situations for our alcohol or drug use and related problems.

Impaired Control

Impaired control means we drink or use drugs in ways in which we did not intend. We cannot always determine when or how much we will use or when we will stop. For example, we decide to stop at a bar for just one drink after work but end up getting nearly drunk and staying late. Or we might smoke all of our dope in one evening when we wanted to save some for the next day. We use more often at inappropriate times or places and behave in ways that trouble us and concern others. For instance, we may drink or use at work, before an appointment, or early in the day. Perhaps we become verbally or physically abusive, inappropriately flirtatious or sexual, or engage in illegal activities while under the influence of alcohol or other drugs.

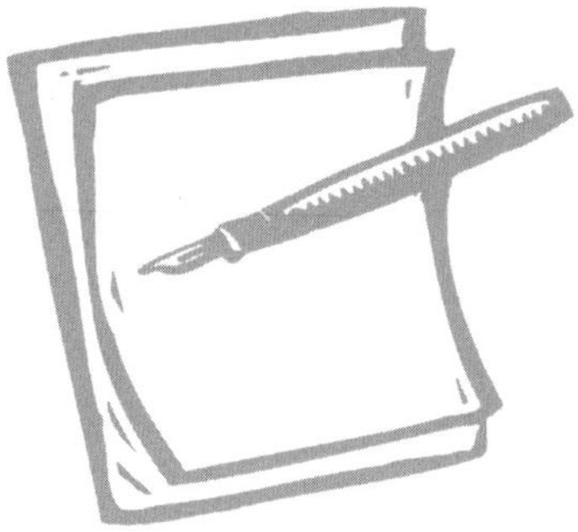

Identify three *significant* situations when you drank or used more than you had planned.

1.

2.

3.

List three *significant* situations when you used alcohol or other drugs at inappropriate times or places.

1.

2.

3.

Continued Use Despite Harmful Consequences

In the crucial phase, we become more dependent on alcohol and other drugs to feel good or to cope with pain. For most of us, our use damages our relationships. We feel bad about ourselves and our behavior as our addiction progresses. Eventually, chemical abuse affects our work.

What consequences have you had in relationships, with your own emotions, and at work while continuing to use?

Relationships: Consider arguments, broken promises, embarrassing moments, breakups, separations, divorces, disappointed or scared kids. Be specific.

1.

2.

3.

Emotional: Consider increased feelings of guilt, shame, embarrassment, fear, anxiety, depression, anger toward yourself. Be specific.

1. ....

2. ....

3. ....

Work responsibilities: Consider time off, tardiness, decreased productivity, diminished thinking skills, missed opportunities or advancements. At home: Consider parenting issues, chores, housework, cooking, handling bills and checking. Be specific.

1. ....

2. ....

3. ....

Unsuccessful Attempts to Limit or Stop Use

After a significant negative consequence, we often attempt to limit our use or even quit. We might try to limit our drinking or drug use by consuming only a certain amount, using only on weekends, or never drinking before evening. Perhaps we try to drink only wine or beer. Maybe we try to substitute alcohol or pot for crack or heroin in order to regain control. Unsuccessful attempts to limit our use or stop completely signal that we're losing control and the disease is progressing.

Unsuccessful attempts to limit our use or stop completely signal that we're losing control and the disease is progressing.

Describe two significant attempts to change or limit your use of alcohol or other drugs and the result.

1. Attempt ....

Result ....

....

2. Attempt ....

Result ....

....

Alcohol- and Drug-Centered Behavior

As our disease progresses so does how much and how often we rely on alcohol and other drugs to make us feel better. More of our time is centered on using chemicals, leaving less time for other areas of our lives. Without knowing it, we become more concerned with how other activities will interfere with our drinking and drug use, rather than how drinking and drug use interferes with our lives.

Describe three ways your behavior has become more alcohol and drug centered. Consider your isolation from your family and friends, your lack of social activities, missed work, neglected finances, infrequent prayer and meditation, and avoidance of religious or community involvement. Be specific.

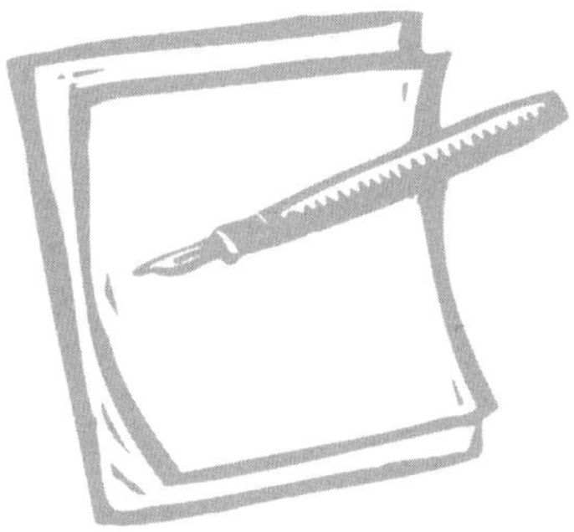

1. ....

2. ....

3. ....

Chronic Phase

Earlier, in the definition of addiction, we talked about *chronic* as "lasting forever." However, in defining the third phase of addiction, chronic means something altogether different. Here the word *chronic* refers to deterioration, the last stage of addiction before insanity or death. Severe deterioration in body, mind, and spirit signal that we're in this phase. Key symptoms include binges, value conflict, physical dependency, and significant emotional and spiritual pain. Not everyone reaches the chronic phase of addiction.

Binges

Bingeing means that we use much more alcohol or other drugs for longer periods and often experience more consequences. When we binge, we are losing more and more control and are becoming more dependent on alcohol and other drugs.

Value Conflict

As our addiction worsens, we act in ways that conflict with our value system. Value conflicts might include lying, manipulation of personal and business finances, not showering or dressing, isolating or leaving our loved ones for hours to days while using, stealing, dealing drugs, exchanging sex for drugs, and forgery to name a few.

Physical Dependency

By the chronic phase, physical dependence is common. Withdrawal symptoms appear when we are without alcohol or other drugs for several hours or longer, depending on the drug. Withdrawal from alcohol or other sedatives, stimulants, and narcotics vary. Signs of withdrawal range from shaky hands, nausea or vomiting, sweating, anxiety, depression, fatigue, unpleasant dreams, increased appetite, insomnia or excessive sleepiness, muscle aches, and fever.

Significant Emotional and Spiritual Pain

Our spirits and emotions take a beating from the repeated assault on our brains from addictive drugs, as well as from related consequences and losses. Depression, anxiety, loneliness, emptiness, hopelessness, despair, self-hatred, fear, and paranoia are our companions in this phase. We become emotionally and spiritually bankrupt. If you have reached the chronic phase, addiction has already torn the very fabric of your life.

Have you experienced symptoms in the chronic phase? If so, describe which ones.

....

....

....

....

CONCLUSION

Addiction is not just a primary, chronic, genetic, progressive, and fatal disease. It is also a treatable disease. The progression of the disease can leave us and our lives in shambles. It can leave us feeling hopeless and helpless. Facing our addiction can be painful. But by doing so, we begin recovery. We move from denial to honesty, shame to self-respect, fear to courage, and despair to hope.

You can begin recovery at any point in the progression of this disease, even if you have moved into the chronic phase. Your body, mind, and spirit have an incredible capacity to heal. Healing occurs once we quit using alcohol and other drugs and seek connections with recovering people, family, friends, professionals, and a Higher Power. Healing occurs through the Twelve Steps of Alcoholics Anonymous.

Do you have a sense of hope that you can recover from this disease?

1	2	3	4
No	*I'm not sure*	*I'm getting there*	*Yes, I have no doubt*

THE TWELVE STEPS OF ALCOHOLICS ANONYMOUS

1. We admitted we were powerless over alcohol—that our lives had become unmanageable.
2. Came to believe that a Power greater than ourselves could restore us to sanity.
3. Made a decision to turn our will and our lives over to the care of God *as we understood Him*.
4. Made a searching and fearless moral inventory of ourselves.
5. Admitted to God, to ourselves, and to another human being the exact nature of our wrongs.
6. Were entirely ready to have God remove all these defects of character.
7. Humbly asked Him to remove our shortcomings.
8. Made a list of all persons we had harmed, and became willing to make amends to them all.
9. Made direct amends to such people wherever possible, except when to do so would injure them or others.
10. Continued to take personal inventory and when we were wrong promptly admitted it.
11. Sought through prayer and meditation to improve our conscious contact with God *as we understood Him*, praying only for knowledge of His will for us and the power to carry that out.
12. Having had a spiritual awakening as the result of these steps, we tried to carry this message to alcoholics, and to practice these principles in all our affairs.